FASCISM AND CITIZENSHIP

THE WEIL LECTURES ON AMERICAN CITIZENSHIP

THE UNIVERSITY OF NORTH CAROLINA PRESS
CHAPEL HILL, N. C.

THE BAKER AND TAYLOR COMPANY, NEW YORK

OXFORD UNIVERSITY PRESS, LONDON

MARUZEN-KABUSHIKI-KAISHA, TOKYO

EDWARD EVANS & SONS, LTD., SHANGHAI

D. B. CENTEN'S WETENSCHAPPELIJKE BOEKHANDEL,
AMSTERDAM

FASCISM
AND
CITIZENSHIP

BY

GEORGE NORLIN
PRESIDENT OF THE UNIVERSITY
OF COLORADO

CHAPEL HILL
THE UNIVERSITY OF NORTH CAROLINA PRESS
1934

PREFACE

A FRIEND who was good enough to read the manuscript of this little volume remarked that he did not fully grasp what I was driving at until he came to the last sentence of the last page. That remark has prompted this word of explanation at the outset.

These lectures had for their immediate background my personal experience of the Hitler revolution in Germany. I was "guest professor" in the University of Berlin for some months before and after Hitler came into power. By a curious irony, I was lecturing on American liberalism at a time when liberalism in all its forms was being driven out of Germany by the Nazi movement.

The experience was of course intensely interesting and, so far as it touched me personally, not unpleasant, thanks to German hospitality. But it was distressing beyond words to be in the midst of a collapsing civilization and to feel underneath the outward demonstrations of mob-ecstasy a nation's tragedy—a tragedy starkly real, yet so fantastic as to seem utterly unreal.

It was impossible not to be shaken and dismayed by that incredible phenomenon. Was civilization, which it took centuries to build, after all a flimsy structure? If such a frenzy could seize upon so stable and conservative a people as the Germans, what nation could think itself immune? Our own?

That feeling was accentuated by conversations with Americans on the voyage home and after my home-coming, when I found that many of my countrymen were receptive to Hitler propaganda and that not a few of them, being convinced that democracy was on the rocks in the United States as well as elsewhere, looked upon Hitlerism (or something like it) not only as a life-boat to take refuge in but as, perhaps, the one ship of state which could navigate our troubled waters.

Such loose thinking regarding Fascism abroad, such amazing lack of appreciation of the meaning and value of our American heritage, could not but suggest the danger that lurks in a shallow Americanism. In a world where nationalism is almost everywhere rampant and militant, the lack of a deeply-rooted and well-considered national consciousness in our country may well be a serious one. Such a consciousness would seem worth striving for if only to serve as an effective quarantine against virulent propaganda from abroad. But it would have a greater value as a basis for that national concert of action which our disjointed, not to say dismembered, domestic situation seems to make mandatory; and perhaps it would have a still greater value as a means of integrating and enriching our isolated, individual lives. Besides, it might help us even to play a better part in world affairs.

The word nationalism is now discredited, at least to some of us, by the excesses of nationalism. Fascism, and especially Hitlerism, is nationalism carried to mad extremes. It is destructive of the greatest values of human life —destructive in the long run, I believe, even of itself.

But, although nationalism in its extreme is a manifest evil, one may nevertheless plead that there is a golden mean of nationalism without which no nation can best promote the good life of the people who compose it. In other words, there is a good nationalism—a proper nationalism.

Such a nationalism has nothing to do with racial prejudice, with national arrogance, with contempt for other nations and races, or with the sublimation of war as the divine business of a chosen people.

Nor has it, necessarily, anything to do with national self-sufficiency (*Autarkie*), economic or otherwise. Doubtless the building of commercial walls has harmed the whole world; doubtless the well-being of all nations would be promoted by a free exchange of goods. But one may hold that view and yet agree that in a world where foreign markets are firmly locked away or at best treacherous and precarious, a nation may find it expedient to look primarily to its own market and seek independence of conditions abroad which are completely beyond its direction and even beyond its influence, especially if "national economic planning" must be the order of the day. It should, moreover, be clear even to the most naïve mind that economics and politics are indissolubly wedded in the world of here and now, and that our country may not sit aloof from the councils of the nations, refusing to mix in their affairs, without subjecting itself to economic isolation. We cannot have our cake and eat it too.

What, then, is a proper nationalism? It is the purpose of these lectures, after dwelling by way of introduction on nationalism at its worst, to approach an answer to this question.

G. N.

Boulder, Colorado
September 11, 1934

FASCISM AND CITIZENSHIP

I

ABOUT a year ago, Selma Lagerlöf made a radio address from Stockholm to the American people. She closed with these words: "I have faith that over there in the great daughterland of the West, the most beautiful dream of old Mother Europe will find its fulfillment."

A gracious greeting from one of the noblest spirits of our time, none the less gracious because it sounds like a voice of long ago. It recalls Goethe's *"Amerika, du hast es besser,"* or William Cullen Bryant's eloquent picture of our country as offering to the oppressed of all nations a greater freedom, a better justice and a more abundant life. Perhaps Selma Lagerlöf was thinking of her own childhood when there was in Europe, as she said, "a veritable America fever," for which the only cure was to set sail to the land of promise. Or she may have been cherishing wistfully still something of the hope of a better order in the Old World when Woodrow Wilson came across the Atlantic with "healing in his wings," before the United States had disowned the League of Nations and placed it, a foundling, upon the doorstep of Europe.

Certainly she was not voicing the general European feeling of 1933, and still less would her words express that of 1934. For Europe has, at the moment, no such hope or faith in us. She has given us up and, in a degree, turned her back upon us. She judges our civilization largely by tales of gangsters, kidnapers, and lynchings; by the films of Hollywood, by the so-called realism of Theodore Dreiser, and by the caricatures of Sinclair Lewis. Our pursuit of dollars, our worship of the business man, has always seemed barbaric. It is true that our prosperity has inspired envy; our material power has compelled respect. But now we have not even these titles to distinction, and Europeans see little reason for courting our good will.

And we, for our part, seem to have had enough of Europe. Our mixing in trans-Atlantic affairs has been disenchanting in its results. We fought with Europeans a war to end all wars, only to find ourselves living now, to use the words of Mr. Frank Simonds, not in a post-war period, but in a pre-war period. We

4

fought with them to make the world safe for democracy, with the result that Fascism is spreading in Europe, and that "liberalism" is being more and more contemned as "that stinking corpse." We associated ourselves with the Allied Powers when they had reached the limit of their resources, and we turned the scale in their favor, only to find now that the feeling towards us is, if anything, more friendly among those whom we helped to defeat than among those whom we helped to victory. We lent great sums of money to the Allied Powers, which they expected to collect from Germany, only to find the war debts in the end transferred to the shoulders of the American people. In more senses than one, therefore, we Americans feel that we lost the war, and we are determined not to be losers again by mixing in foreign affairs.

I am speaking, not of men like Nicholas Murray Butler, who are still valiantly preaching a generous internationalism, but of the general disillusionment. We, too, are turning our backs. Will Rogers' remarks (February 15) apropos of the civil war in Austria and the threat that all Europe might leap to arms are indicative of the popular mind. "Mr. Franklin D., shut your front door to all foreign ambassadors. . . . Just send 'em these words: 'Boys, it's your cats that's fighting. You pull 'em apart.' "

Washington's and Jefferson's admonitions are now more than ever laid to heart. Indeed we would go further than they. Jefferson said: "Peace, commerce and honest friendship with all nations—entangling alliances with none." But many of us, and among them economists, favor a national isolation which would mean complete independence of treacherous foreign markets. A popular book, *Self-Contained America,* urges with much plausibility that we trade amongst ourselves alone and let the rest of the world go hang—a sentiment which is reciprocated across the Atlantic. Mr. John Maynard Keynes, of all people, has at length been caught in the tide of national self-sufficiency, and now declares himself against "economic entanglements." "Let goods," he says, "be homespun wherever it is reasonably and conveniently possible." Apparently this is thought reasonably and conveniently possible almost everywhere, if tariffs, subsidies and embargoes mean anything. *Sinn Fein,* for our-

6

selves alone, has become the watchword of nations. "The world," says Professor Rogers of Yale, "is fast becoming a series of walled estates, not unlike those of the Middle Ages."

For this state of affairs, we have ourselves partly to blame. But it is idle to speculate now as to what might have been if, instead of immuring ourselves, we had taken our place in a commonwealth of nations. The fact with which we have to reckon is that internationalism is discredited by its abortions and that the world is taking refuge in an intense nationalism, of which Fascism is but an extreme form.

II

Hitlerism in Germany is especially instructive, and I shall take a few moments to discuss that curious phenomenon. When the Germans laid down their arms in 1918, their humiliation was tempered with hope in Wilson's Fourteen Points. They, who had been schooled in the authoritarian state, set up the Republic in order to be in favor with those who fought to make the world safe for democracy. They, who had felt themselves a people set apart, made an honest attempt to enter a world fellowship. They, a warlike race, were ready to renounce war. *"Krieg Nie Wieder,"* was a sentiment heard in Germany, as in other countries. They, who had been a heel-clicking, goose-stepping people under the Empire, painted the word *Freiheit* in great letters on the roadside rocks, where it remains to this day, and gave free scope to liberalism, internationalism and pacifism.

They were hopeful at first under this baptism of freedom, only to experience the frustration of their hopes. Half starved at the end of the war, thousands upon thousands of them were literally starved to death after the armistice by the continuation of the food blockade during the months while the peace conference in Paris deliberated on the terms of peace. They were written down in the Treaty of Versailles as the criminal among the nations and saddled with the cost of the World War. They staggered desperately under a load of reparations to be paid, not in goods, but in gold. They suffered the humiliation of the invasion and occupation of the Ruhr Valley by French and Belgian armies in time of peace. They resorted in their extremity to a policy of inflation which got beyond control and ruined millions of the great middle class. They had embraced liberalism only to suffer from the excesses of liberalism. They found themselves divided under the parliamentary system, not into two or three great political parties, but into some thirty political factions, with no party having at any time a decisive majority, so that the only government possible under the Republic had to be based from time to time upon loose coalitions of parties and factions in the *Reichstag*. Not only that, the very integrity of the Fatherland was threatened by Communists, who took their orders from Moscow and boasted that they were citizens, not of Germany, but of the world international.

Under these circumstances, they were unable to deal effectively with domestic affairs—with growing economic distress and unemployment. Above all, they were helpless to carry out a vigorous foreign policy—that is, to lift themselves out of the dust of humiliation and stand erect among the nations. They were disarmed by the Treaty of Versailles and reduced to a third-rate power. The chagrin of their disarmament was softened at first by the promise of general disarmament to the German level. But that promise was not kept, nor has a single step been taken in that direction since the Treaty was signed. The Germans have existed as a nation since 1918, not by virtue of their own strength, but on the sufferance of other nations. They have been from the beginning to the end of the Republic a subject people. They have waited for the League of Nations to accomplish their deliverance, and have waited in vain. They have learned by bitter experience that if their chains are to be broken they must do it themselves. The withdrawal of Germany from the League of Nations and from the Disarmament Conference last October (1933) was but the German Declaration of Independence.

The just historian of the ill-fated German Republic will set down many things to the credit of the Republic. I have not attempted a complete picture. I have stressed only those experiences which have associated free institutions in the German mind with defeat, distress and humiliation, and so prepared the soil for Fascist propaganda. Hitlerism is nothing more nor less than an extreme reaction against all the spiritual forces which were unloosed by the revolution of 1918 and which were given free play under the Republic—against the liberalism, internationalism and pacificism which are now conceived to have "stabbed the German army in the back," to have brought the German people to their knees and kept them weak and impotent.

Nothing is more significant of the change which has come over Germany since 1918 than the change in the use of the word freedom. *Freiheit,* in the sense of the word which was blazoned on the rocks under the Republic, is condemned as an anarchic, disruptive, disintegrating force which enslaved the German people and kept them in chains. The freedom which they now glorify in song is the freedom of the German *Reich* to live its own life and work its own will without let or hindrance. And it is this liberation of the State, or of *Das Volk,* through the extinction of liberalism which is the objective of the Hitler movement. Dissent is now the great crime, obedience the great virtue and regimentation the supreme necessity. One people, one soil, one blood, one flag, one party, one rhythm, one thought—that is the ideal of the *Totalitätstaat*.

It is remarkable to what extent that ideal has already been carried into effect. The tremendous power of the Hitler party, with its Brown-Shirt army of twenty-five hundred thousand men, exercised upon an unresisting and, for the most part, an acquiescing people, has wrought miracles of change in a few months.

Politically, Germany has been welded into a unity which she has never known before. All the political parties, save the National Socialist Party, have been wiped out as by a sponge. All the separate states have been merged into the *Reich,* and are ruled by the central Cabinet in Berlin. That Cabinet is absolute in its power. It may play with the relics of republicanism— with elections, plebiscites, *Reichstag* sessions, constitution making—but it may use or discard these forms at will. It is limited by no constitution, by no bill of rights, by no body of laws. Its will from day to day is law. It rules with iron hand an authoritarian state such as no Bismarck ever dreamed of.

In the economic field, the *Totalitätstaat* aims to be a self-contained and self-sufficient state. Germany does not propose to be starved out by a food or munitions blockade again. *Autarkie* is, as will be seen, a general objective of German life in all its aspects, but it is a word used especially of economic self-sufficiency. This is to be attained through *Gleichschaltung,* which is again a key word in the Nazi vernacular. In the economic realm, it means the coördination and regimentation of all production in the interest of the prosperity and power of the *Reich.* Hitler has taken over the great labor unions, the federation of German industries and the agricultural organizations. They are all under his thumb. Theoretically, there is an end to the class war of the Marxian philosophy, to the conflict between group interests, between agriculturalists and industrialists, between capital and labor—all being merged into a state corporation seeking only the well-being of the state. Men in Hitler's Germany are supposed to be no longer workers or employers or capitalists, but Germans working for the Fatherland. It is *Deutschland Ueber Alles* in the sense that the state is everything, the individual nothing save as he

13

contributes to the wealth and might of the nation.

The same exaltation of the state, or of *Das Volk,* as a mystic unity, is seen in the attempt of the Nazis to purge the German population of alien strains and to breed back to a pure-blooded, homogeneous Nordic race. First of all, the Jew must go. The crusaders of the hooked cross have persuaded themselves and others that the Jew is the incarnation of all the disintegrating forces which have brought the German giant to his knees. He is, in Nazi language, a parasitic growth—a "plant louse"—which must be exterminated if the true, creative, warlike, northern stock is to grow into the fulness of its power.

But Hitler's Germany not only has no room for Jews; it has no room for any who do not add to the strength of the *Reich.* Interior Minister Frick of the Hitler Cabinet, objects that a sentimental individualism has squandered much of the nation's resources in coddling the incapable, the crippled, the weak and the infirm, and insists that the nation devote itself to "increasing the descendants of sound heredity." And this is Nazi policy. The programme of the sterilization of the unfit is but one device of an eugenic therapy to be practiced ruthlessly in order that *Das Volk* may be pure, vigorous and strong.

But Hitlerism does not stop there. It has an inexorable logic. It is nothing if not thorough. It is not enough for Germany to be politically, economically and racially a giant unity. It must be a cultural unity as well. It must be regimented under a single *Weltanschauung*—a common emotion, purpose, and philosophy of life. This regimentation has been pushed vigorously ever since Hitler came into power. There was, for example, the great gesture of the burning of the books on the tenth of last May. More recently it has been thoroughly organized and systematized. Last November there was set up, with Dr. Joseph Goebbels, Minister of Propaganda and Enlightenment, at its head, the *Reichskulturkammer,* an elaborate state corporation for the control and direction of all the instruments of publicity and enlightenment which contribute to the moulding of the national mind —books, newspapers, periodicals, magazines, radio, music, theatres, especially the cinema, and art in general, the object being to coördinate all the people into a singleness of heart and mind.

Furthermore, the schools and universities have lost every semblance of academic freedom. They must preach the gospel of the "New Dawn" or come under the ban of the Nazi government. On the sixth of last May, I was present at the convocation in the University of Berlin which marked the impact of the Revolution on one of the great universities of Europe. It was not a red letter day to those who cling to the belief that truth transcends nationality and race; for it was the day of the official inauguration of the Germanization of truth or, as the Nazis call it, "the nationalization of truth." I listened, with what feelings may be imagined, while the Minister of Education, Herr Doktor Rust, laid down the law to "meine Herren Professoren," saying among other things that "unprejudiced, objective, scientific teaching which is blind to the spiritual changes within the nation will no longer be tolerated."

That would seem to mean simply that education must be propaganda. It does mean that, but it means more than that. One cannot begin to understand the "New Dawn" without appreciating that Hitlerism is a retreat from realism and rationalism to a mystical fanaticism. Hitler proudly calls his movement a fanaticism, and Dr. Goebbels calls it, to emphasize its ruthless quality, the "steel romanticism of the Third *Reich*." Reason and intellect are dethroned; and emotion, intuition, impulse reign in their place. Indeed, intellectualism is held in scorn as something pale and unhealthy. It is a thing for pedants and professors, not for red-blooded men.

"We must think with our blood," say the Nazis, which means that thinking must be done, not in terms of dispassionate reason, but in terms of national and racial emotions, aspirations, and prejudices. And it is part of the Nazi program to set up a body of "truth" native to German soil and appropriate to German blood, not intellectual, not academic, but emotional and dynamic—a *Credo* which Germans must be made to believe in order to be saved as a nation and a race.

A primary article of this creed is the dogma of the superiority of the Nordic race and especially of the Germanic stock. A recent Nazi book on anthropology, *Neue Grundlage der Rassenforschung,* by a Dr. Gauch, goes so far as to divide the animal world into Nordics on the one hand and the lower animals, including non-Nordics and conspicuously Jews, on the other. The Nordic race, when uncontaminated by other strains, is extolled as virile, warlike, self-sacrificing and creative. "It and it alone," writes Herr Hitler in his book, *Mein Kampf,* "has produced the creative spiritual strength which by a singular union of brutal fist and cultural genius has been responsible for all the great achievements in art and government."

It is, therefore, part of the great mission of the Hitler movement to purify the race and so release its vital and creative power. To do so is to join forces with the divine will and purpose, which has singled out and chosen this people to flourish, to conquer, to dominate, and to bless the earth.

That is the lesson of the mystery play which was staged a few months ago by the Ministry of Propaganda, entitled *Das Spiel von Job dem Deutschen.* The play draws to a close with the triumph of German arms over the powers of Satan. The angels sing: "Praised be the Lord who loves strength in the strong. Praised be

war, and praised be the victory of the German."
Finally, God Himself speaks to Job: "German,
your line shall be the fountain of the world.
. . . The whole earth will I give you that you
may lead it and rule it to My will. . . . I will
give the earth's glory to your race and from
now on you shall be the race to receive My
revelation. The holiest treasures of mankind
shall be in your keeping."

But what is the purpose of this *Gleichschaltung,* this regimentation of the people in all
these respects—politically, economically, socially, educationally and culturally? There may
be more than one answer to this question, but
undoubtedly the main answer is that the super-
objective of the Nazi party is the welding of all
Germans absolutely together so as to present a
solid front to the rest of the world. The supreme necessity of the Hitler *Reich* is felt to be
Wehrhaftigkeit, the readiness to fight; and the
integrating soul of the "New Dawn" is *Wehrgeist,* the spirit of a soldier nation.

I have tried in this brief fashion to sketch the
Hitler movement as I saw it and experienced it
on the ground. I have tried to speak fairly, not
to say sympathetically. But to attempt to

understand it and so in a degree to condone it is one thing; to approve it is quite another thing. In the last analysis it seems to me to be utterly barbaric. Certainly it is un-Christian. It is no accident that the first outspoken revolt against the movement has come and is coming from the Christian church. Here is a warfare in which there can be no reasonable compromise. Hitlerism spurns the doctrine of the sacredness of the human personality in the eyes of the All-Father, which is the essence of the Christian teaching and the foundation of mutual tolerance and good will. In effect it reverts to the worship of a tribal God, and its feeling of human brotherhood, so far as it exists at all, is narrowed to His chosen people. Its human sympathy is too limited to be wasted on those who are beyond the pale. Its treatment of racial minorities is as brutal in kind as anything in history and would, I fear, be so in degree were it not for fear of world opinion. It was born in hatred and prejudice, and out of such materials it would build love of race and country; and in order to foster that hatred and prejudice, it is the father of lies. It has no conscience, no scruples, in the common meaning of those terms. It regards itself as "beyond good and evil." It has no use for the Sermon on the Mount or for other parts of the Christian Evangel which impede the passions of a war-like race. It renounces, not war, but the renunciation of war; for war is glorified as the supreme, nay, the divine, function of the Fascist state.

III

Hitlerism, then, is nationalism pushed to the last degree. It is a madness, but since it could seize upon a highly civilized people like the Germans, it is an alarming madness. One cannot say where it may not break forth. It is spreading in Europe like a dangerous epidemic. It leaps across the Atlantic. It is here amongst ourselves.

Mussolini once said that Fascism was an Italian product, not for export. Now, however, he speaks of it as having ascended from the national plane to the world plane, and claims for Italy the credit of leading the world to a Fascist civilization.

Mussolini is not given to understatement, but here he speaks the language of events. Liberalism in Europe is, to put it mildly, on the defensive. On this side of the Atlantic, too, it has its back to the wall. Many Americans now regard our faith in democracy as an outworn superstition, and certainly there has been a sharp general decline in what has long been to us a national religion. A hundred years ago, when Bancroft began publishing his monumental *History of the United States,* a history of our Chosen People, no one in our country questioned for a moment that American institutions not only had wrought our own salvation but were "the way, the truth and the life" for the rest of the world. That enthusiasm has been a long time cooling off. In 1916, there was delivered in the House of Representatives a remarkable speech, of which the peroration is interesting enough to quote: "Mr. Speaker, I have an abiding and an unbounded faith in the great destiny and in the undying glory of my country. I believe that the time is not far distant when we shall have complete military and naval, economic and industrial, intellectual and spiritual preparedness; when American genius and American influence will dominate the nations and overshadow the earth; when our Constitution and our Declaration of Independence will be the mould and model of free institutions among all the tribes of men; when the torch of freedom which was lit at the flame of the American Revolution will be a beacon light to the oppressed of all mankind; when our soldiers and our sailors will be feared and respected on every land and on every sea; when the drum beat of our country will be heard around the world; when freedom's flag will illumine all the skies; and, whether proceeding from the mouth of an ambassador or from the hot throats of Federal guns, the mandate of the great Republic will be heard and obeyed throughout the earth." [1]

Indeed, as late as 1925, Mr. Coolidge in his inaugural address set forth less dithyrambically but not less assuredly his faith in the saving grace of American institutions: "It is in such

[1] *Congressional Record*, Vol. 53, p. 12679.

contemplations, my fellow countrymen, . . . that I find ample warrant for satisfaction and encouragement. . . . The past and present show faith and hope and courage fully justified. Here stands our country, an example of tranquillity at home, a patron of tranquillity abroad. Here stands its government, aware of its might, but obedient to its conscience. . . . America seeks no earthly empire built on force and blood. No ambition, no temptation, lures her to thought of foreign dominions. The legions which she sends forth are armed, not with the sword, but with the cross. The higher state to which she seeks the allegiance of all mankind is not of human but of divine origin. She cherishes no purpose save to merit the favor of Almighty God."

But, when Mr. Coolidge was thus giving voice to his fervid Americanism, the "debunking" of American life had already begun. In 1922, there appeared a book, edited by Harold E. Stearns, written by thirty American critics under the title, *American Civilization,* which was really an attack upon American barbarism. The next year, H. L. Mencken launched his submarine, the *American Mercury,* designed apparently to sink every craft freighted with American ideals and aspirations. The word *idealism* became a by-word, not to say a hissing. No one dared to write a pleasant book, hardly a decent book. We basked our souls, not in the sunshine, but in the shadows of our existence. With the help of our smart intellectuals we ridiculed and satirized and bespattered America, past and present. We transmuted our idols into clay, if not into mud. We regarded ourselves, if I may use such a paradox, with supercilious contempt. We felt ourselves no longer a chosen people but a lost people. Indeed, we seemed to find a perverse satisfaction in being lost. We welcomed and bought by the millions the novels of Sinclair Lewis, and saw in America only *Gopher Prairies* and *Babbitts*. In a word, we gave ourselves over to a prolonged debauch of self-criticism and self-disparagement which was so extreme in both quality and quantity as to have been called by one of our writers "the Eighth Wonder of the World."

That orgy has, fortunately, largely spent itself from sheer satiety, save in one respect. We cannot talk with a friend without being told, we cannot pick up a book or a magazine without seeing it in print, that democracy has failed. Most of this is, I dare say, loose talk. Democracy has not failed—relatively. It is fair to remember that the American Republic has withstood the assaults of time and change at least as well as any polity in history up to now. And it is well to remember also that the alternative to democracy, call it by whatever name you will, is tyranny. Is tyranny a better thing? "Tyranny," says Herodotus, "disturbs ancient laws, violates women and kills men without trial; but a free people, ruling themselves, have in the first place the most beautiful name in the world, and in the next place they do none of these things." But that is a voice from long ago. Is tyranny a better thing now? Ask the Jews in Germany. Ask the thousands upon thousands of political dissenters in the prison camps of Germany. Ask the myriads of refugees from Germany. Ask the men and women in Germany who cherish in their hearts a freedom which is no longer theirs.

But those of us who have not lost faith in democracy, who dare not lose faith in democracy, who feel that there are things more precious than life itself and that the chief of these is freedom, may not be too complaisant about the future. Our democracy is staggering under the impact of a monstrous industrialism which we may not be sure that we can tame, direct, and control for our own good. We have a stupendous job on our hands. We must somehow bridge the perilous gap between extreme plenty and extreme want. We dare not drift on *laissez faire*. We must furnish at least the necessities of life to more than one hundred and twenty millions of human beings, if not as a measure of justice or of mercy, then as a measure of our own safety. *Ubi panis ibi patria,* is the very truth. We cannot exist as a nation, half replete and half hungry. Neither can we exist as a nation, half at work and half idle. For idleness is as demoralizing as hunger. The machine is spewing out goods, but devouring the work of human beings. Education for leisure, now so popular as a theme of exhortations, is not enough. The curse which drove man out of Eden to earn his bread by the sweat of his brow has now become a birthright for which men are willing to march and fight. We must distribute a reasonable amount of creative, productive work over a self-respecting population. And this is by no means a simple under-taking!

Whether any government on earth can do all this, remains to be seen. Certainly our democracy now confronts its greatest task and its greatest test.

IV

But the fact that democracy is now in its greatest crisis is no good reason for the feeling which I encounter in not a few of my fellow countrymen that the latest fashion in government is one to which we must ourselves resort sooner or later if we would keep our civilization a going concern. What is it that Fascism can do that a republic cannot do? What, indeed, are the claims which are commonly made for Fascism?

Well, for one thing, we are told by our tourists returning from Italy that under Mussolini the trains are run on time, swamps are drained and roads are built. But is the Fascist state the only one in which trains are run on schedule, roads built and land reclaimed? Do not free men, too, do these things?

But, it is urged, Fascism with its *Führerprincip* ensures the real leadership which an efficient government these days must have, in contrast to democracy, which allows only mediocre men to come to the top. If for leadership we substitute drovership, the claim must be allowed. But are Mussolini in Italy and Hitler in Germany more competent as leaders than MacDonald in England and Roosevelt in America? And are the troubled waters out of which dictators emerge a safer source from which to draw our rulers than the suffrages of a free people? Then there is the problem of succession to think of. Mr. Stanley Baldwin in a recent broadcast in England said that Fascism is like a great beech tree in that nothing upstanding grows in its shade; subservience, submission, docility, yes, but not a future leadership.

Again, it is argued that Fascism substitutes prompt action for dilatory debate in a world which is gasping for breath under a flood of words. Beyond question, the demands upon the machinery of government are now so daily and hourly insistent that we must shift emphasis from an over-deliberate parliamentarism to a greater centralization of responsibility and power. But cannot democracies move in that direction without ceasing to be democracies? And have the discretionary powers which our own republic has delegated to a Lincoln, a Wilson, or a Roosevelt proved inadequate in times of stress? In fact, American democracy has learned through experience to trust less and less to the legislative branch, which is the scene of pulling and hauling by local interests, and more and more to the chief executive, who represents the whole people.

Finally, it is alleged that Fascism wipes out all internal friction and creates a smoothly running coöperative state. Indeed, it is the supreme boast of Hitlerism that it has done this. It has compelled all factions, all parties, and all classes to compose their discords and march together under the hooked cross to the rhythm of *Deutschland Ueber Alles*.

But has it? Has Germany really been made

over by terrorism and strong-armed propaganda into one great happy family?

On paper all is well. Class conflict has been driven into exile in company with the Marxian philosophy. There is but one party, the National Socialist party, and one people marching and working as one man for the Fatherland—on paper.

But in reality there are now two classes in Germany, the one underprivileged, the other privileged. There are, on the one hand, the people in general and, on the other, a Brown-Shirt population. If there be any doubt about the latter's being the privileged class, consider alone the fact that special Nazi courts have been set up for the trial of Brown offenders.

Furthermore, the Hitler party itself can hardly be called a unity. It is supposed to fix its eyes on one thing only—the good of the Fatherland. But the Hitler party has its left and right wings and its center. The good of the Fatherland is one thing to the radical down-and-outers of the left, who have very human feelings about the distribution of wealth; it is quite another thing to the industrialists and the Junkers of the right, who have seized upon

Fascism as a weapon to put down socialism, communism, and labor unionism; and it is still another thing to the conglomerate middle class of footless or discontented students, clerks, craftsmen, shopkeepers and small farmers, who all demand their place in the sun.[1]

Hitler is riding, not one horse, but many horses. Can they all be made to run neck and neck into the promised land? Up to now, it appears that industry and big business have the inside track; not the workers, certainly. One of the first things done by Hitler when he came into power was to demolish the elaborate, mutual-welfare structure which had been built up by the labor unions through the efforts of fifty years. The justification for doing so was simple. Where all are brothers working for the Fatherland under a government which coördinates the interests of all classes, no group has need to organize to fight its own battles and press its own cause. The cause of one is the cause of all.

That sounds very well, too well, perhaps. At any rate, it remains to be seen whether any such

[1] This statement has been amply confirmed by more recent events.

group as the working class is better off under a government where it has neither voice nor liberty of action or in a democracy where it is free to organize and agitate for its due place in the social order.

Mr. Hitler sneers at American democracy as being in reality a plutocracy. But, granted that money has been known to buy its way into the seats of power in a democracy, is it less able to do so under a dictatorship? Mr. Hitler, so far, does not appear to have been too rough on geese that lay golden eggs.

In sum, it has not yet been proved by human experience that a government which punishes agitation, dissent and opposition as treasonable crimes is the best instrument for the promotion of the general welfare. There is still something to be said for the English liberal tradition under which the government in power addresses minority parties as "His Majesty's most loyal opposition."

V

It seems a bit ironical, in a State which holds the birthplace of Andrew Jackson, to pause to examine the claims of a polity which wages war on democracy—a polity which, though it is the latest fashion, is not even a new fashion. It is new only in its technique. It repudiates violently the philosophy of Magna Charta, of the French Revolution, of the American Declaration of Independence. It harks back to the Middle Ages, and beyond. The great sweep of civilization in the modern age has been away from it.

That is, perhaps, no final reason why we should not turn backward. But at least the burden of proof is on those who would have us think that the slow struggle of centuries—the battles fought and the blood shed—has been in a vain and empty cause.

The breakdown of the republics which were brought forth on the European continent by the Great War proves little or nothing, so it seems to me, as to whether the difficult ideal of democracy is desirable or practicable of attainment. They were so prematurely born as to have been almost still-born. The German republic, especially, was doomed from the first by the circumstances which attended its birth. Where it failed, no form of government could have succeeded. Had Hitler come into power in 1918, Hitlerism would be today a tale that is told.

As to our American democracy, should it break down in this crucial period, it will be not because it has not long been rooted in a congenial soil, not because it has been compelled to grow in the ashes of humiliation and defeat, not for lack of abundant and varied resources, not for lack of a fairly intelligent and enterprising citizenship, but for the lack during two generations now of the devotion of our best intelligence to the common good. Perhaps it is well that our democracy is now undergoing its supreme trial and that we are being roughly shaken by a sense of personal insecurity and danger out of our habitual political apathy, indolence and indifference. Life has been too easy for us. We have had a good-natured tolerance of corrupt or stupid politics because in spite of them or along with them our own getting has been good. We have not been tried enough, we have not been toughened enough, by hardship and danger. We have lived softly, and we are soft. Let me here recall a picturesque statement made many years ago by Fisher Ames of Massachusetts, if only to object to it. Comparing monarchy and democracy, he said: "A monarchy is like a merchantman, you go on board and ride with wind and tide in safety and elation, but by and by you strike a reef and go down. But democracy is like a raft, you never sink, but, damn it, your feet are always in the water." This amusing metaphor may contain a measure of truth, but in fact our feet have not always or often been in the water. We have had relatively smooth sailing—too smooth for our own good. We have been for the most part lounging passengers, not members of the crew trimming the sails, manning the pumps, and keeping a sharp lookout. Since the stern discipline of our pioneering experiences, prosperity—the easy ravishing of a virgin continent—has engendered a drifting easy-goingness, a fatalistic optimism, which cannot stand up in a gale. At any rate, our morale collapsed abjectly in the storm which broke upon us in '29.

What we are going through now seems to have crashed upon us suddenly, but in reality it has been coming upon us for a long time. Twenty-five years ago, Mr. Herbert Croly was writing convincingly of the perils in the ease of our material success. In his very interesting book, *The Promise of American Life,* he said: "For two generations and more the American people were, from the economic view, most happily situated. They were able in a sense to slide downhill into the valley of fulfillment. Economic conditions were such that, given a fair start, they could scarcely avoid reaching a desirable goal. But such is no longer the case. Economic conditions have been profoundly modified and social problems have been modified with them. . . . The same results can no longer be achieved by the same easy methods. Ugly obstacles have jumped into view, and ugly obstacles are peculiarly dangerous to a person who is sliding downhill. The man who is clambering uphill is in a much better position to evade or overcome them. Americans will possess a safer as well as a worthier vision of their national promise as soon as they give it a house on a hill-top rather than in a valley." [1]

The way down into the valley has been, according to Mr. Croly, the way of economic self-seeking and national irresponsibility; the way up out of the valley is through a devoted nationalism; not that individualism and localism need to be wiped out, but that they can now be given significance and worth only through a social vision and effort which are national in scope and character.

That view was a daring heresy when Mr. Croly set it forth in 1909. Today it is, I suppose, an accepted doctrine. "The whirligig of time and of events," says the internationalist, Alfred Zimmern, "has made us all nationalists now." We have become so by a process both of broadening and of limiting our social vision. We have come to think perforce in terms, not so much of the individual, or of the family, or of the community, as in terms of the nation. In the nineteen-twenties we thought we were thinking in terms of the world. But our not too happy adventures in internationalism have

[1] Quoted by permission of The Macmillan Company, publishers.

driven us back upon ourselves and made Sinn Feiners of us all in greater or less degree. President Roosevelt, in his inaugural address, insisted that it was the business of the American people first of all to "set their own house in order." That is the business of every nation. Every people is being schooled by experience to work out its own salvation primarily through national, not through international, coöperation.

That is, no doubt, to many of us who have dreamed of a world fellowship or a world federation a distressing sentiment. It seems like a retreat, not an advance. It seems that the logic of blind events, not that of a directing intelligence, is impelling peoples toward a condition, if not an ideal, of *Autarkie*—of the self-contained and self-sufficient nation.

But it may be that we have been over-precipitate in our zeal for a world order. Perhaps we have put the cart before the horse. Perhaps, as Mr. Zimmern thinks, the way to a proper internationalism is through a proper nationalism.

Indeed, as things are now, a proper nationalism—a golden mean of nationalism—would seem to be the best quarantine (or should I say

the best antitoxin?) against the virulent nationalism of the Fascist movement.

Even Fascism, which is nationalism gone
wild, has its good points—its virtue. It seeks
to wipe out individual and factional strife and
merge all classes in the solidarity of the nation.
It is, in Aristotelian phrase, vicious only in its
excesses. One cannot under any other supposi-
tion begin to understand how Hitlerism among
a people like the Germans is accepted as a
means of national rehabilitation. At any rate,
I venture to think that we ourselves may draw
instruction from it both as to what to do and as
to what not to do.

I suppose that it is not open to debate that
the movement towards national coördination has
grown out of necessities which are felt on both
sides of the Atlantic. The Germans have
revolted against the excesses of individualism,
and so have we. In our own vernacular, a too
"rugged individualism" has become a too
"ragged individualism." And we, too, seek the
remedy through a degree of national regimentation.

In his inaugural address, Mr. Roosevelt said:
"If I read the temper of our people correctly,

we now realize, as we have never realized before, our interdependence on each other; that we cannot merely take but we must give as well; that if we are to go forward, we must move as a trained and loyal army willing to sacrifice for the good of a common discipline, because without such discipline no progress is made, no leadership becomes effective. We are, I know, ready and willing to submit our lives and property to such discipline, because it makes possible a leadership which aims at a larger good. This I propose to offer, pledging that the larger purposes will bind upon us all as a sacred obligation, with a unity of duty hitherto evoked only in time of armed strife."

I mean no disparagement of the earnest words of the President when I say that Fascism abroad talks the same language. There are, of course, tremendous differences between what I may call Hitlerism abroad and Rooseveltism at home. The one is destructive of freedom; the other strives to give it content and meaning. The one relies in the last analysis on force, the other on persuasion. Let us not be confused. We can delegate vast powers to the chief executive of the nation and trust to his leadership, and still be free men. Indeed, to do so may be the only effective means of preserving our freedom.

Nevertheless, the Roosevelt administration marks a change which is for us more radical than is Fascism for Europeans. I mean a change in our attitude towards government. We have been in the main jealous and distrustful of government. Those who settled our country came here, most of them, to escape from oppression. They had come to look on government as something not their own, as something put upon them; and when they set up their own government, it was upon the principle that that government is best which governs least. That principle served well enough for the simple life of a frontier existence, but it soon betrayed its limitations. "Everybody for himself and the Devil take the hindmost" tended to destroy the very freedom of which it was a crude expression. As Woodrow Wilson put it in his first inaugural address: "We reared giant machinery which made it impossible that any but those who stood at the levers of control should have a chance to look out for themselves." Little by little, therefore, the power of organized society, of the national government especially, has been invoked to make personal freedom for the many something more than an empty word. And at the moment we are experiencing a degree of social regulation and control which Thomas Jefferson would have found unthinkable, and which we ourselves would have found unthinkable not long ago. Only six years ago the President of the United States Chamber of Commerce made an address, entitled *A Plea for Inefficiency in Government,* urging that a strong, competent government "eats holes in our liberties." Now we have by Act of Congress created a stronger government than we have ever known in time of peace, and we are trusting that government to patch the holes in our liberties.

It is common to speak of the New Deal as representing a new American revolution. It is not, however, at all revolutionary in its underlying principle. Mr. Roosevelt has proposed simply to restore the Ancient Truths which, he complains, have been driven out of our Temple. The philosophy of the New Deal is the philosophy of Woodrow Wilson, of Theodore Roosevelt, of Abraham Lincoln, of Thomas Jefferson, of the Declaration of Independence, of the "American Dream," about which I shall speak later. The New Deal is radical in method only in that it represents a sharp accentuation of a gradually awakening consciousness that the American principle or the American philosophy has in effect broken down from our excessive dependence upon individual and local effort and for lack of a national concert of action—for lack, that is to say, of a proper nationalism. The "pioneer" virtue of "neighborliness," of which Mr. Roosevelt is so fond of speaking, must extend itself to the boundaries of the nation.

We may be able some time to think in terms of the world as one great neighborhood. But in the face of our own difficulties and with nationalism rampant everywhere on earth, that is a dream for the future. Indeed, it would seem that the greatest service we can render to the world in this time of crisis is to set our own house in order and look to the quality of our own nationalism.

For this, it is not enough to set up a new code or even a multitude of codes. The insufficiency of so doing has grown painfully manifest during the past few months, during which self-seeking has seized upon the letter and ignored the spirit of the New Deal. The change in technique is not sufficiently motivated by a change of heart.

VI

The complaint is often heard that Mr. Roosevelt is taking advantage of his powers to propagandize the nation—that he is another Hitler. I am no partisan, pleading for the infallibility of the present administration, but I do not share in that complaint. I am painfully aware of the tyranny which lurks in the mass psychology which the enormous machinery of propaganda is creating in Europe. But Mr. Roosevelt has been very reasonable in the use of the power which is delegated to him, and if I were to make any complaint it would be that not enough has been done by way of spiritual integration in preparation for changes and readjustments which have been so largely and so suddenly attempted. The New Deal was inaugurated in a time of extraordinary mental and moral disintegration. The American people were like Stephen Leacock's cowboy who "rushed from his cabin, leaped upon his horse and rode rapidly off in every direction." On every hand was scattered the wreckage of ideas and dogmas, but there was no common vision, no common direction. Mr. Roosevelt, at the outset of his presidency, urged that "if we are to go forward, we must move as a trained and loyal army willing to sacrifice for the good of a common discipline." But something more than a word of exhortation now and then is necessary if anything like the New Deal is to succeed. We must do nothing less than build up a national rhythm, a national conscience, a national *esprit de corps* as a fundament to any general and fruitful concert of action.

I would even go so far as to take a word out of Hitler's mouth and urge the necessity for Americans of a *Weltanschauung* of their own. I have, of course, no sympathy with the movement in Germany to smother individuality by coercion in the realm of the spirit. The attempt which is being made there to take seriously the game of national make-believe, to build up a body of mythology and call it the nationalization of truth, impresses me merely as nationalism run amuck. But there is, as I have suggested, such a thing as a golden mean of nationalism, a reasonable concert of purpose, of feeling, and of thinking—a community of culture, a national soul.

Herr Oswald Spengler, in his recent book, *The Hour of Decision,* declares that the United States is in this sense neither a real nation nor a real state, since its life is organized exclusively from the economic side and consequently lacks depth. Such a criticism puts us uncomfortably on the defensive, but we may justly demur to so sweeping an indictment. We are not merely a nation of shopkeepers. We have a national tradition, a national history of our own, which is certainly no less worthy than that of any European country, though we are as a people only dimly aware of what I dare call the glory of our own past. We have developed out of our experiences national traits which are, I believe, deeper than any dollar-chasing philosophy, though we are rather inarticulate both in our talk and in our thinking about them. We have a national soul, of which we are too vaguely conscious and which is too often obscured by trumpetings of mere sound and fury, and perhaps still more in recent years by an equally intemperate self-detraction.

Would it be merely academic to urge that our teachers and our writers and all who have their part, great or small, in the shaping of our national mind would now at least best serve the nation by bringing clearly into the foreground of our consciousness what Americanism truly is, if only that our people may step more securely into the uncertain future from a footing in their living past?

We would, I suppose, not all agree as to what Americanism means. To Big Bill Thompson, it means Anglophobia and twisting the lion's tail forever. To Sinclair Lewis, it means *Gopher Prairie* and *Babbitt*. To Upton Sinclair, it means the exploitation of human beings. To H. L. Mencken, it means the crudities and imbecilities which have been played up monthly in his magazine, under the caption, *Americana*. To Henry

Ford, it means, doubtless, bigger and better mass production. To Madison Grant, it means a triumphant Nordism, whatever that means. And so on, and so on.

But such interpretations are, I dare say, mostly the surface froth and bubbles on a deeper national undercurrent which moves silently on, though we are hardly conscious of it because we are in a sense so familiar with it, even as we are hardly conscious of the air we breathe.

If, then, I speak of familiar things, and nothing new, it is with the conviction that it is things familiar, though vaguely felt and apprehended, which require renewed emphasis and definition if we are to be in the fullest and richest degree a nation.

VII

What, then, is Americanism? First of all, it is a peculiarity of Americanism that it looks, not so much backward, as forward to the future. Our pride is not so much in past performance as in the "glory of the unfinished." "America," said Franklin Lane, "is an aspiration. America is a spirit. It is the constant and continuous searching of the human heart for the thing that is better."

It is easy for the cynic to make sport of this quality: it has so often bodied itself forth in utopian soap-bubbles, which have been most gorgeous at the point of their collapse; it has so often expressed itself in noisy, clamorous ways, not only in the bombast of the platform, but in our literature as well—in, for example, the occasional blatancy of Walt Whitman's great visions of democracy or in the rattling lines of Vachel Lindsay:

"I am Kallyope, Kallyope, Kallyope,
  Tooting hope, tooting hope, tooting hope, tooting
    hope,

Shaking windowpane and door
With a crashing cosmic tune,
With the war cry of the spheres,
Rhythm of the roar of noon,
Rhythm of Niagara's roar
Voicing planet, star and moon,
Shrieking of the better years." [1]

Yet such excesses are but the fortissimo of something in our sober selves, something which we have come by honestly, something our very own, from which, perhaps fortunately, we cannot escape without ceasing to be Americans.

I have quoted already from Mr. Croly's *The Promise of American Life*. Permit me to quote again: "American life cannot with impunity be wrenched violently from its moorings any more than the life of an European country can; but our American past, compared to that of any European country, has a character all its own. Its peculiarity consists not merely in its brevity, but in the fact that from the beginning it has been informed by an idea. From the beginning Americans have been anticipating and projecting a better future. From the beginning the

[1] From *The Kallyope Yell*, by permission of The Macmillan Company, publishers.

Land of Democracy has been figured as the Land of Promise. . . . An America which was not the Land of Promise, which was not informed by a prophetic outlook and a more or less constructive ideal, would not be the America bequeathed to us by our forefathers. In cherishing the promise of a better national future the American is fulfilling the substance of the national tradition."[1]

Undoubtedly the American habit of projecting a better future, to use Mr. Croly's phrase, has been at low tide since the war. For its flood tide, we must go back to the middle of the last century, to the period which Lewis Mumford, in his brilliant book, has named *The Golden Day.* An English visitor to America at that time, Alexander Mackay, wrote this observation about us: "Other nations boast what they have been, but the citizen of the United States exalts his head to the skies in the contemplation of what the grandeur of his country is going to be. Others claim respect and honor because of things done by a long line of ancestors. An American glories in the achievements of a distant posterity."

[1] By permission of The Macmillan Company, publishers.

That comment has in it a bit of humorous extravagance, but it is essentially true. You will find quite the same thing in our own writers of the time—in Thoreau, in Melville, in Whitman, in Emerson. Emerson, for example, in his *Young America,* spoke of this as a "country of beginnings, of projects, of vast designs and expectations. It has no past; all has an onward and prospective look."

That was a hundred years ago in the heyday of the robust, exuberant, romantic, hopeful, faithful America. Has America now grown old? I wonder. To put the question more definitely, I juxtapose two poems, dealing with the eternal question of the significance of our human life. One is by our contemporary, Edwin Arlington Robinson:

"No, Ben," he mused, "It's nothing. It's all nothing.
  We come, we go; and when we're done, we're
    done. . . .
  Spiders and flies—we're mostly one or t'other—
  Your fly will serve as well as anybody.
  And what's his hour? He flies and flies and flies,
  And in his fly's mind has a brave appearance,
  And then your spider gets him in her net,

And eats him out and out and hangs him up to
    dry.
That's Nature, the kind Mother of us all.
And then your slattern housemaid swings her
    broom,
And where's your spider? And that's Nature
    also.
It's Nature and it's nothing. It's all nothing.
It's a world where bugs and emperors
Go singularly back to the same dust
Each in his own time; and the old, ordered stars
That sang together, Ben, will sing the same
Old stave tomorrow." [1]

The other poem is by Emerson:

"I am immortal. I know it. I feel it.
Hope floods my heart with delight.
Running on air, mad with life, dizzy, reeling,
Upward I mount—faith is sight, life is feeling,
Hope is the day-star of night.
Chance can not touch me. Time can not hush me.
Fear, hope, and longing at strife
Sink as I rise, on, on, upward forever.
Gathering strength, gaining breath—naught can
    sever
Me from the Spirit of Life."

There is a vast difference. The future then

[1] Quoted from *Ben Jonson Entertains A Man From Strat-
ford*, by permission of The Macmillan Company, publishers.

was a rainbow, now it is hidden in clouds. Is Emerson's, then, the voice of America drunk; and Robinson's, that of America sober—sober with years and disenchantment?

I venture to say that Emerson's lines come nearer being our authentic voice. The strong wine of a national romanticism to which Emerson and Whitman gave literary expression has entered into and warmed our very blood. Futilitarianism, defeatism are foreign to our nature. It may seem to be the goddess of Cynicism who sits enthroned in our Temple, but beneath her grinning mask are the features of Hope.

I mentioned in my first lecture a rather devastating picture of American civilization, edited by Harold E. Stearns. Mr. Stearns for some years sought a more congenial climate in Europe, but has now, as it were, repatriated himself and has published a book, *Rediscovering America*.

In this he speaks of the gusto of American life, its hopeful exuberance, which he now finds rather engaging. "One may call this," he says, "illusion if one likes . . . but it is the American way, and it adds immeasurably to the thrill and color of existence. To be always assailed by doubts and reservations may be the mark of intelligence and discrimination, but it is the surest way known to put a blight over the fun of being alive. Americans would like to be drunk with the wine of life all the time, and as we have very strong constitutions, generally speaking, I see no good reason why we should not be. In this sense, I should much prefer to go through life drunk all the time, as the healthy and successful American is, than sober all the time as the not-too-healthy and not-too-successful European." [1]

I have been reading with intense interest what seems to me to be one of the best fruits of our American civilization. I refer to the systematic, well-considered attempt over a period of years to arrive at a national concert of thinking regarding a proper *Weltanschauung* to be presented in our schools, now formulated in a *Charter for the Social Sciences,* drafted by Charles A. Beard.

One of the paragraphs of that Charter is a sober declaration of faith, which is pertinent here. It does not sound altogether Beardish, but may be none the less significant on that account.

[1] By permission of the Liveright Publishing Corporation.

"Underneath all . . . national ideals is a belief that the lot of mankind can be continuously improved by research, invention, and taking thought. That is the philosophy of progress, and, if rightly conceived, is one of the noblest conceptions yet conceived by the human mind. The environment and conduct of men and women can be modified by effort in the light of higher values and better ends. Human relations, constitutions, economic arrangements, and political practices are not immutably fixed. If there is anything which history demonstrates, it is this generalization. All legislation, all community action, all individual effort are founded on the assumption that evils can be corrected, problems solved, the ills of life minimized, and its blessings multiplied by rational methods, intelligently applied. Essentially by this faith is American civilization justified."

VIII

But if our people think largely in terms of the promise of American life, that does not mean that our thinking is not rooted in the past—in our own past. Emerson's statement that America has no past was even at that time a rhetorical exaggeration. We have, no less than the older nations of Europe, a tradition and a history of our own—a past which is distinctive and unique, not in its brevity, but in its quality; I might even say, in its worth. And yet we are, for the most part, unschooled in the value of our proper heritage. We have thought of our history defensively as homespun, in contrast to the ornate tapestries which are supposed to form the backgrounds of European civilizations.

Homespun it is, but with a strong and honest fibre; and, strangely enough, it is only in recent years that we have begun to grasp its real significance. It was not until 1893, when Professor Turner began to publish his epoch-making studies on the significance of the frontier in American history, that it began to dawn upon

us that what is most distinctive in our history is
not what we have mostly read in our histories,
not even the battles we have fought in blue or
grey or brown, important as these are, but the
battle with the wilderness—the Two Hundred
Years War to conquer and possess a continent,
not by professional armies marching to the blare
of trumpets and the rattle of drums, but by
homespun pioneers who advanced not only beyond the outposts of civilization but, for the
most part, beyond the protection of the flag,
hewing their way through wild forests, tram-
pling underfoot the hostility of savages, fighting
their own battles, building their own settlements,
setting up their own governments, helping
themselves and helping each other and develop-
ing through this experience and this discipline
the qualities of self-reliance and self-respect, together with a spirit of neighborliness, of mutual
good will—qualities which have entered into
the very blood and bone of the American
character.

That is the American Saga, the American
Odyssey, matchless in its scope and character,
no mere congeries of myth and legend, yet a
romantic cycle, vital with human interest—with

dread and hope, frustration and triumph, comedy and tragedy, prosaic drabness and high adventure, nay, even with the stuff of poetry.

Miss Harriet Martineau, an intelligent Englishwoman, writing about us in the eighteen-thirties, recognized the true quality of pioneering America when she spoke of the "embryo poet" in the American people, meaning essentially what Lewis Mumford means when he characterizes our westward adventuring from frontier to frontier as "romanticism in action."

Unfortunately for literature, it was not a singing romanticism. The pioneers were poets (*poietae*) only in the primary sense of that Greek word. They *made* Odysseys, and they made a nation. But Homeric bards were lacking then, and they have been lacking even unto this day.

It is a strange fact that, with a few notable exceptions, this tempting material has been and is neglected by American authors. The rich store of a national legacy is ours for the taking and using, but the American authors who are most read at this moment draw their material from China or from the world at large.

We have had during the past two decades

what some critics call a native literature. At least our writers have been compelling us to gaze upon ourselves and our inadequacies as a nation. It has been a disconcerting experience. Some of us have found comfort in Tolstoi's discovery that one who looks at himself in a mirror appears less engaging than he really is. But, on the whole, the discipline has been good for us; it has served as a national catharsis; it has purged us of vain conceits. Humility has not been an outstanding American quality, and yet it is one of the graces, and perhaps one of the virtues as well. But it may be questioned whether a national self-criticism is an adequate cement of a national fellowship. It is to be preferred, I think, to the overweening sense of national superiority which Fascism deliberately breeds. But there is a golden mean between looking down upon ourselves and looking up to ourselves which comes from contemplating not only the shadows but the quickening sunlight of our past and present. The literature of deflation has gone far enough. There is more need now of expanding the sound spiritual currency of the nation.

Fortunately, the raw materials of our national

Odyssey are being collected with devoted care in some of our university centers and made ready to be woven into the texture of a national history and, let us hope, of a national literature and culture.

The full picture remains to be made, but certain colors are already manifest, though not always clearly seen because of the over-emphasis which has been given to the crudities of the frontier.

A friend of mine, for a time an instructor in the University of Colorado, wrote a little poem, *Out Where the West Begins,* which has been very popular in my neck of the woods. I quote it in part:

"Out where the hand clasp's a little stronger,
  Out where the smile dwells a little longer,
  That's where the West begins.
  Out where the sun is a little brighter,
  Where the snows that fall are a trifle whiter,
  Where the bonds of home are a wee bit tighter,
  That's where the West begins.

          .   .   .   .   .

  Out where the world is in the making,
  Where fewer hearts in despair are aching,
  That's where the West begins;
  Where there's more of singing and less of sighing,

Where there's more of giving and less of buying,
And a man makes friends without half trying,
That's where the West begins."

Mr. Chapman, in these lines, was distilling his feeling about the Rocky Mountain West. But the West did not begin there. In fact, the distinctively American West began with the movement of our people from the lowlands of the Atlantic seaboard to the upland slopes of the Appalachian Mountains, while yet they hardly dreamed of surmounting that formidable barrier. And since then, the West has "begun" again and again and again, until near the close of the last century the census report of 1896 officially declared the American frontier a thing of the past.

It is, as you know, the thesis of Professor Turner that every "west" has represented a revolt against oppressive conditions and a rebirth of democracy—a rebirth, I may say, of the humanism which Mr. Chapman has caught and bodied forth in his poem.

Mr. James Truslow Adams, following Professor Turner in the main, has written a very excellent book, *The Epic of America,* the epic of what he calls the "American Dream"—a dream of escape from a narrow, stifling, hedged-in existence to a freer, fuller, richer life for every man.

That dream has marched with the American people across the continent from the rising to the setting sun. It has been thwarted again and again. Wherever the "cake of custom" has grown hard and fixed, wherever society has grown stratified, wherever industrialism has put machinery above life, and profiteering above humanity, the dream has ceased. But again and again and again that dream has been renewed on every American frontier, and flooded back from west to east, until it has become a part of the American temperament and character.

There have been many frontiers in America where men have adventured and dreamed the American dream. But we may single out certain frontiers which have played a signal part in the making of the nation. The first frontier produced the humanism of Jefferson and the Declaration of Independence. Then, in the cynical reaction which followed the Revolutionary War, the dream languished for a time, until the second great frontier, west of the mountain barrier, gave to America a new recognition of the worth and dignity of the common man, which we find expressed in the teachings of Emerson and Whitman, in the elevation of a commoner, born and bred on the frontier, to the presidency of the republic, and in that stirring of the national conscience which produced, among other humanistic reforms, common schools and state universities for poor and rich alike. The third great frontier gave us Abraham Lincoln and the Gettysburg Address. In a large degree it gave us the *United* States, not the Balkan States, of America, and it gave us not only a nation, but a nation in which human bondage was no longer sanctified by law. The last frontier, or the last West, in which I was born and bred, sent forth that humanistic protest against exploitation by big business and commercial buccaneering, which, ridiculed at first as wild-eyed populism, was made respectable and, in a degree, effective in Theodore Roosevelt's principle and programme of "A Square Deal For Everybody." And Roosevelt, it may be remarked, while a child of the East, had been a ranchman on a Dakota frontier. Mr. Bryan, the protagonist of that rebellion, was, perhaps, a bit rhetorical in that remarkable oration of his which almost carried him into the

President's chair, but he was of the company of
Jefferson and Lincoln when he said in that oration to eastern capitalism:

"When you come before us and tell us that
we are about to disturb your business interests
by our course, we reply that you have disturbed
our business interests by your course. We say
to you that you have made the definition of a
business man too limited in its application. The
man who is employed for wages is as much a
business man as his employer; the attorney in a
country town is as much a business man as the
corporation counsel in a great metropolis; the
merchant at the crossroads is as much a business
man as the merchant of New York; the farmer
who goes forth in the morning and toils all
day, . . . and who by the application of brain
and muscle to the natural resources of the country creates wealth is as much a business man as
the man who goes upon the board of trade and
bets on the price of grain; the miners who go
down a thousand feet into the earth or climb
two thousand feet up the cliffs and bring forth
from their hiding places the precious metals to
be poured into the channels of trade are as much
business men as the few financial magnates who

in a back room corner the money of the world."

There speaks the last American frontier. There speaks every American frontier. And there speaks, I dare say, the voice of America, as we now stand on a new spiritual frontier, questing still for the realization of our dream.

IX

I have found it convenient to use the term, American Dream, even though it may suggest a degree of insubstantiality or even of footlessness in American aspiration. It has, indeed, often been somewhat nebulous in the popular mind. But it has been none the less at times a very dynamic force. It has even "struck a spark in the Old World," to use the phrase with which Lord Morley characterizes the impact of the American Declaration of Independence upon the Bourbonism of Europe. Certainly it is the heart of the American tradition. It is, as Mr. Adams says, the "chief motif of the American Epic" and gives to the American Epic its distinctive quality.

It has again and again formulated itself in definite terms. Its great historic formulation is in the philosophy which forms the introduction to the Declaration of Independence. But it may be said to be greater than any formula which it has framed, larger than any mould into which it has sought to pour itself. It may be roughly adumbrated as the quest of the human spirit to find or to create a soil and climate where men may grow and flower and be fruitful each in his own way and according to the capacity of each.

It is not, of course, exclusively American. But it is American in the sense that upon this continent it has had (and may I add, still has) greater scope for action and fulfillment. It is informed by the Christian evangel of our common brotherhood and of the inviolate sacredness of human personality. It is Roger Williams' doctrine of "soul liberty"—of the divine right of the soul to live its own life and think and speak its own thoughts and to be unhampered in its endless searching for the truth. Indeed, it may be said to rest not only on the postulate of our common humanity, but on that of our common divinity.

"It is," said William Ellery Channing, "because I have learned the essential equality of men before the common Father that I cannot endure to see one man establishing his arbitrary will over another by fraud or force or wealth or rank or superstitious claims. . . . It is because I see in man a great nature, the divine image, and vast capacities, that I demand for him means of self-development, spheres for free action; that I call upon society not to fetter, but to add to his growth. Without intending to disparage the outward, temporal advantages of liberty, I have habitually regarded it in a higher light, as the birth-right of the soul, as the element in which men are to put themselves forth, to become conscious of what they are, and to fulfill the end of their being."

Even our first secular formulation of the American Dream was more than secular: All men are created equal, they are endowed by their Creator with certain unalienable rights;

among these are life, liberty, and the pursuit of happiness; to secure these rights, governments are instituted among men, deriving their just powers from the consent of the governed—these are not mere statements of fact; they form a declaration of faith.

Jefferson called the Declaration an expression of the American mind; and so it was, and so, I presume to add, it is. It must be confessed, however, that much has been done to confuse the American mind as to its meaning. There have been the vaporings of politicians; and there have been, no less, the detractions of cynics. Some have dismissed the Declaration of Independence as a campaign document, useful for its time and purpose. A chief justice of the Supreme Court once decided that it was limited in its application to a superior race and class. An American ambassador at the Court of St. James has characterized it as a thing of "glittering generalities." A distinguished American scholar and writer has said cavalierly that declaring that men are created equal did not make it so—as if Jefferson and his colleagues did not know that!

Jefferson, himself, gave the key to the intended

meaning of that document when he said shortly before his death: "I have always believed that the mass of mankind was not born with saddles on their backs, nor a favored few booted and spurred to ride them legitimately, by the grace of God." And Lincoln, in the second great crisis of our history, spoke the last word upon this question when he said that the authors of the Declaration "meant to set up a standard maxim for free society which should be familiar to all, and revered by all; constantly looked to, constantly labored for, and even though never perfectly attained, constantly approximated, and thereby constantly spreading and deepening its influence and augmenting the happiness and value of life to all people of all colors everywhere."

If I have ventured to say a word about the significance and worth of this charter of our liberties in our American *Weltanschauung,* it is because there are sinister forces in motion to consign it to our historical archives where, resting in dust and peace, it may agitate us no more. The whole philosophy of Fascism is violently at war with its principles. Even liberalism is doubtful of its further validity. I read, for example, in a very persuasive book, entitled *A Realist Looks at Democracy,* by Alderton Pynk, an English liberal who weighs liberalism critically in the balance, these words: "In an age of privilege and despotism the new ideas of equality and liberty were necessary and vital. Their power overthrew empires and re-drew the map of Europe. Those ideas, and the ideas of representative government with which they are connected, have since become sufficiently trite to be apprehended by a half-educated populace, but in a twentieth-century world they have lost their vital force. At the time of the Bourbon monarchy it was above all things necessary to assert one aspect of the truth, namely, that nobleman, priest, and peasant were equal in virtue of their common humanity; today it may be just as necessary to call attention to another aspect of the truth, namely, that in virtue of their natural endowments men are fundamentally unequal."

I am not able to follow this reasoning. In the first place, no one with any intelligence, no Jefferson or Lincoln and, I dare say, no one even of the half-educated populace, has ever doubted that in their endowments men are unequal. All that has been insisted upon is that such endowments as men have should not be cramped and crushed by organized society, but should be given due freedom of expression and growth by the social organism. In the second place, the age of "privilege and despotism" is not now behind us but upon us again. Fascism in Germany repudiates insolently and brutally our common humanity. Jews, for example, are not human; they are beyond the pale. Racial prejudice and intolerance is lifting its hydra heads all over the world. This of all times is the very time to plead, with Walt Whitman, that "men are more alike than not like, more noble than not noble." And let it not be forgotten that to repudiate the worth of other human beings is to forfeit the claims of our own humanity!

X

Again I come back to a golden mean of nationalism. There is room in a proper nationalism for the American Dream, for the doctrine of Roger Williams, for the principle of divine right which is laid down in the Declaration of Independence, and which is written into the bill of rights of every state constitution and of our national constitution as well. I mean the doctrine that there is a realm in which the individual human being is sovereign in his own right, in which he is free to think and speak his own thoughts, to live his own life, and to pursue his own spiritual and material well-being, without let or hindrance so long as he does not trespass upon the rights of other men—a realm or domain which no person, no society, no government may invade, for this is sacred ground.

That is Americanism in its true sense, which is still worth fighting for and, if need be, dying for now that it is threatened by mad forces without and loose thinking within. There is the sovereignty of the nation and there is the sovereignty of the individual soul. One sovereignty may not destroy the other without destroying what is distinctively precious in American civilization.

XI

These two sovereignties, if I may be allowed such an expression, pulled together without much driving in the pioneer days when a man on his isolated farm was almost literally monarch of all he surveyed, before American life became as complicated as a traffic jam in New York. To yoke them together now into a proper concert of action is as difficult as it is necessary. How difficult it is, is manifest in Mr. Roosevelt's heroic attempt at regimentation by persuasion in his programme for economic rehabilitation. It will be quite as difficult when we squarely face, as we must, other equally insistent problems such as—to speak only of one of the most pressing —that of at least equalizing, and perhaps of enriching, educational opportunity throughout the nation.

Public education is a cherished fruit of the American Dream. Now that free land is a thing of the past, it is the most effective device to give every one a fair chance. And yet because public education is largely a very local enterprise, because we have no national educational system but 127,000 separate educational principalities, the equalization of educational opportunity remains a dream unrealized. The youngster in a country school is underprivileged as compared with the city boy or girl. And at this moment there are hundreds of thousands of American children who have no schools at all to go to. To say, under these conditions, that all our people are equal in respect of educational opportunity is to speak sheer nonsense.

The situation is complicated by the fact that the responsibility of providing for the public welfare through agencies of health and education is relegated to the several states, while the nation is draining by almost every device of taxation the sources of public revenue. What, for example, is more anomalous than the situation in which the state university now finds itself? It is in fact, at least in the service it renders, not a local institution, not a state institution, but a national institution. The University with which I am connected, for example, sends forth its trained graduates more widely through the nation at large than do those universities which are thought of as being more national in their character and scope. And yet to support a university which serves the nation we must pick the already depleted pockets of a local population.

I can see no adequate remedy in the long run other than through a proper nationalization of educational policy. I have been impressed by the note of warning which has been sounded by my friend, Henry S. Pritchett, of the Carnegie Foundation, as to what this might mean. "Thousands of public school teachers," he said, "would, under such a dispensation, be hot in their pursuit of their Congressmen. What this sort of pressure would do to the public treasury would make the advocates of the soldiers' bonus seem modest in comparison." I must confess, however, that as I contemplate with distress the economic status of the teacher and the professor in the public schools and colleges of our land today, the prospect of a reasonable pressure exerted upon Congressmen or others does not strike terror into my academic soul.

XII

I come now to an aspect of the American Dream which has not, I think, been adequately appreciated. I will call it, for want of a better term, its out-of-doors quality. Professor Tyler, in his great *History of American Literature in the Colonial Period,* has shown at length "the curiosity, the awe, the fresh delight" with which the early colonists, coming from a world in which nature was clipped and trimmed and artificialized and, as it were, crowded out by human occupation, gazed for the first time upon the unspoiled beauty of the New World. One remembers also the words of William Penn, written from his retreat in the Pennsylvania forest: "Oh, how sweet is the quiet of these parts, freed from the troubles and perplexities of woeful Europe."

And one of the forces, by no means the least potent, which impelled the American people to move westward from frontier to frontier, to settle like butterflies, now here, now there, only to flit on again when overtaken by civilization, was the lure of the open, the prospect of elbow-room in the unpreëmpted wilds.

Professor Turner quotes in this connection Kipling's lines:

"We were dreamers, dreaming greatly, in the man-stifled town,
We yearned beyond the sky-line where strange roads go down."

And we may recall the case of the naturalist, John Muir, who could find his way anywhere in the wilds, but in the crowded city streets was as confused and bewildered as a lost child. The story is told of him that one day in San Francisco he stopped a stranger and asked, "What is the quickest way out of town?" "But where do you want to go?" said the stranger. "To any place that is wild," he replied.

That is an extreme instance of something that is peculiarly American. John Muir was a product of the pioneer tradition. So also are the multitudes who each year make pilgrimages to our great national parks or "to any place that is wild." And so also are the millions who every summer pack their bedding and their camp kits into the covered wagons of this day and roll along from countryside to countryside.

> "They tour from Memphis, Atlanta, Savannah,
>   Tallahassee and Texarkana,
> They tour from St. Louis, Columbus, Manistee,
> They tour from Peoria, Davenport, Kankakee.
> Cars from Concord, Niagara, Boston,
> Cars from Topeka, Emporia, and Austin,
> Cars from Chicago, Hannibal, Cairo,
> Cars from Alton, Oswego, Toledo,
> Cars from Buffalo, Kokomo, Delphi,
> Cars from Lodi, Carmi, Loami.

> *   *   *   *   *

> Ho for Kansas, land that restores us
> When houses choke us, and great books bore us!
> While I watch the high road
> And look at the sky,
> While I watch the clouds in amazing grandeur

Roll their legions without rain
Over the blistering Kansas plain—
While I sit by the mile-stone
And watch the sky,
The United States
Goes by." [1]

A competent psychiatrist of my acquaintance attributes much of the nervous disorder which seems increasingly to afflict American life to the urbanization which thwarts and turns back upon itself the pioneering instinct which has been fixed in the American temperament by two centuries of continuous questing for freedom and elbow room. That may be an overstatement of the case, but certainly the piling up of our population in cities has done violence to the American temperament and is inimical to a wholesome American civilization.

In this connection it may be interesting to say a word about a trend of thought on the European continent. The countries which are most urbanized and industrialized look with wistful envy upon those parts where life is less crowded, simpler and happier, as in the Scandinavian

[1] Quoted from Vachel Lindsay's *Santa Fé Trail*, by permission of The Macmillan Company, publishers.

countries, where if there is less wealth, there is also less poverty. Writers like Spengler insist that life becomes deranged when divorced from the soil, and this idea has been caught up by Fascism. Mussolini revives the policy of Caesar Augustus and fosters agriculture. He has not found his Vergil to hymn the praise of country life, but is taking practical measures to curb what he calls the "monster of industrialism." Hitlerism in Germany turns away from the artificialities of so-called civilization to what it calls *Kultur,* using this term in the sense of a simple, natural life associated with the countryside—with woods and rivers and lakes and mountains and flowers and growing crops. Civilization in this way of thinking is what one finds in cities: smoke and crowds and noise; tramways, motor cars, elevators, mechanisms— all the artificial devices which complicate, confuse, enervate and even pervert human life. Life in cities is deracinated, sophisticated, and parasitic rather than creative. Hence the attempt now being made to root life more and more in the countryside, to marry *Blut und Boden,* to rehabilitate agriculture, to plant schools outside of cities, to encourage in every way pilgrimages of city youth into the open country, and even to create through the bold programme of Walther Darré, their Minister of Agriculture, a peasant aristocracy—a nobility rooted in the soil.

This has the doctrinaire thoroughness which is so characteristic of the German mind, but it seems to me to have a measure of truth. There is truth in the old Greek feeling for Earth as the Great Mother from whose apron strings we break away at our peril, or in the legend of Antaeus, whose giant strength became as nothing as soon as he was lifted off the ground.

And this truth is, I venture to say, particularly vital for American democracy. Democracy with its essential quality of "neighborliness"—of good will—does not flourish in tenements, and still less in flats. It requires room and sun. Here I would call attention to a book by George Santayana, which deserves to be better known, *Character and Opinion in the United States*. "If it were given to me," he says, "to look into the depths of a man's soul and I did not find good will at the bottom, I should say without any hesitation, 'You are not an American.'" Santayana is here speaking of a quality engendered by the roominess of pioneer life. "The optimism of the pioneer," he insists, "is not limited to his view of himself and his own future: it starts from that; but feeling assured, safe and cheery within, he looks with smiling and most kindly eyes on everything and everybody about him. Individualism, roughness, and self-trust are supposed to go with selfishness and a cold heart; but I suspect that that is prejudice. It is rather dependence, insecurity, and mutual jostling that poison our gregarious brotherhood. . . . The milk of human kindness is less apt to sour if the vessel that holds it stands cool and separate."

I must own up to a temperamental prejudice in this matter. I confess to a thrill whenever I read in Crèvecoeur's *Letters of an American Farmer* of the "resurrection" experienced by our early immigrants on escaping from cramped conditions in Europe and taking root in the larger and vitalizing soil of the New World. I nod approval to Jefferson's lyrical declaration of faith in the self-respecting farmer, who draws not only his sustenance but his virtues from the largess of the soil, and so is the safe custodian of our democratic ideals. And I quite agree with Walt Whitman when he writes: "Democracy most of all affiliates with the open air, is sunny and hardy and sane only with nature. American democracy in its myriad personalities, in factories, workshops, stores and offices—through the dense streets and houses of cities, and all their manifold sophisticated life—must either be fibred and vitalized by regular contact with outdoor life and air and growths, farm scenes, animals, fields, trees, birds, sun-warmth, and far skies, or it will certainly dwindle or perish."

But if all this is not mere sentiment, then democracy in America has been on the wane for some time, and it should not cause too much lifting of the eyebrows to urge that the prime necessity of American culture (not to use the word civilization) is a concerted effort to restore American life so far as may be to the countryside and to make the existence of our rural population alluring and not repelling, as it is now. Jefferson called "those who labor in the earth the chosen people of God, if He ever had a chosen people." Were he living today, he would see in them a lost people, or, shall I say, a forgotten people?

It may be purely academic to talk about that now. I appreciate the force of Professor Beard's remark that "Jefferson's America of free and up-standing farmers ruling the country in liberty has been turned upside down by steam and machinery. Ten million teachers singing the praises of agriculture would have been powerless to block that inexorable march."

Perhaps so. Perhaps we are confronted by a condition and not a theory. Or perhaps we are confronted by both a condition and a theory. We have not merely drifted into this topsy-turvy condition upon an irresistible tide. We have brought it upon ourselves. I will not say with John Maynard Keynes that "we have until recently conceived it a moral duty to ruin the tillers of the soil and destroy the existing human traditions attendant on husbandry, if we could get a loaf of bread thereby a tenth of a penny cheaper." That is putting it rather strong. But Professor Beard himself would be the first to say that our national planning, so far as we have had any, has neglected agriculture in favor of other things, nay, has let the power to tax, which is the power to destroy, rest with crushing force on the farmer, and that Shays's Rebellion and the contemporary uprisings of the agrarian West have been revolts against a real injustice. If agriculture is our basic creative industry, as we say it is, and as in fact it is, then it is high time that we put first things first, not last, if anywhere.

I am not thinking now only of Mr. Alvin Johnson's *Happy Valley*, watered by some Merrimac, Susquehanna, Tennessee, Willamette, Colorado, or other river as beautiful as its name, where he proposes, half playfully, half seriously, to settle our five thousand unemployed Ph.D.s and provide for their reëducation. That prospect is not without its allurement to one who has been all his life, like Horace, *jam, jam futurus rusticus*. But I am thinking also of the plight of what Mr. Johnson calls, not too prettily, the "corn-and-hog-wallows of America."

The attempt which is now being made under the New Deal to turn the overflow of cities countryward, to give factory hands a bit of land to delve in, to provide subsistence homesteads, and to put those who have labored in the soil on their feet is altogether admirable and should enlist the self-interest, if not the conscience, of the nation. But even this attempt has a curious emphasis, which betrays the fact that even now in our thinking the farmer is incidental, not first in our concern. There is much talk of the necessity of "gearing agriculture to industry," none of gearing industry to agriculture. Read, if you will, the prologue to the Agricultural Adjustment Act. It is not stated therein that the purpose of the Act is to restore the farmer to his due place and status in the nation's quest of the good life. Rather it is the purpose of the Act to restore his purchasing power so that he may be a stimulant to industry.

I am, I suppose, quibbling about words, but it does seem that the revolution which produced the New Deal has not gone far enough. We are valued, all of us—farmers, professors, and the rest—for our purchasing power, not for what we can contribute to the culture of the nation. In this regard, I must say that Fascism, much as I abhor it, is a step ahead of us.

It would be, of course, merely silly to want to take from industry its due place in the sun. All that is desired is that it should not obscure the sun. The most ardent lover of the countryside is no more revolutionary than Robert Frost's *Lone Striker,* who one day let the factory do without him and sought refuge in an upland wood:

"He knew a path that wanted walking;
He knew a spring that wanted drinking;
A thought that wanted further thinking;
A love that wanted re-renewing.
Nor was this just a way of talking
To save him the expense of doing.
With him it boded action, deed.
The factory was very fine,
He wished it all the modern speed.
Yet, after all, 'twas not divine,
That is to say, 'twas not a church.

.　　.　　.　　.　　.

But he said then and still would say
If there should ever come a day
When industry seemed like to die
Because he left it in the lurch,
Or even merely seemed to pine
For want of his approval, why
Come get him: they knew where to search."

XIII

I have now touched upon the heart of the American tradition, which is worthy, I believe, to be cherished as the heart of our national culture. That is not to suggest that we follow the lead of German Fascism in its extreme attempt to create a completely isolated *Weltanschauung* —in its attempt, that is to say, to hedge itself about with walls of prejudice which may prove to be, not shelters, but prisons of the mind. "Ideas, knowledge, science, hospitality, travel— these," says Mr. Keynes in his essay on *National Self-sufficiency,* "should of their nature be international." Yes, by all means, provided that one's mind and heart be rooted somewhere. There is always danger that this sort of internationalism be spun so thin as to be without substance. We are all acquainted with the inverted snobbery which looks up to every country but one's own, with the pious fraudulence which loves mankind but not one's own kind, and with the utter tawdriness of a commercial cosmopolitanism which is rooted only in the impulse to hawk its wares over the world. Nothing is more shallow and desolate than what Mr. Alfred Zimmern calls a deracinated internationalism. Better a narrow nationalism than that. But there is, as Mr. Zimmern so convincingly points out, a good nationalism—a consciousness of fellowship in a national heritage, tradition and culture—which can give depth and warmth and expansiveness to our individual being without setting up barriers of prejudice against the world at large. And all that I am urging here is that there be a core of native feeling and thinking in our national consciousness to give vital substance and meaning to the phrase, *Americanus sum;* to furnish a common rhythm to our marching together against menacing conditions within our borders; and to provide for our common defense, not in the military sense alone, but in the sense of a spiritual armament strong enough to expose the American mind to bracing winds that blow over the world, while fortifying it against storms that threaten to uproot civilization itself.

The necessity of preserving and enriching this core to form a broadly American *Weltanschauung* calls for concert of action no less than do the imperatives of our economic and political life. Here, however, we find ourselves in great perplexity and difficulty. We encounter at once the protest of the very freedom which it is our purpose to protect and guard. In the commerce of commodities we have been driven by circumstances stronger than our habits to an increasing degree of social regulation and control. In the commerce of the mind and spirit we feel no such compulsion; we cling to *laissez faire;* we even license exploitation. The druggist is inhibited from dispensing dangerous narcotics and stimulants, but there is no inhibition against drugging and debauching the mind. A degree of social regimentation protects our bodies, but the spirit is a fair field for buccaneering.

Mr. Alderton Pynk, in the very interesting book to which I have referred, *A Realist Looks at Democracy,* discusses this anomaly at length, arguing convincingly that democracies dare not longer continue this license, lest they perish from the excesses of liberty. They cannot afford to shut their eyes to the significance of a world momentum toward a national direction and control of culture. They cannot safely harbor disintegrating forces—enemies within the gate—

in the face of the solid front which a menacing Fascism presents.

Mr. Pynk is well aware of the great difficulty of preserving liberty without permitting license. He is repelled by the extreme regimentation of Fascism, but he insists that democracy, to preserve its very life, must even at some risk of going astray move to some middle ground—some golden mean—where freedom shall be vouchsafed to the sincere and honest thinker, writer, or artist to work without let or hindrance, but denied to the pimp and panderer who prey upon the frailties of human nature under the pretense of giving people what they want. It must be a prime concern of organized society to create a tonic atmosphere in which the human spirit is free to attain its largest life. Freedom is, after all, a paradoxical thing. To set no bounds to it may be to suppress it; to set limits may be to give it scope and meaning. When Mussolini had taken over the control of the Italian press, he informed the journalists of Italy that he had made them the freest in the world. In other countries, he said, newspapers were under the commands of plutocratic syndicates or partisan politics or mercenary individuals, and were compelled "to dispense sensational news which produced in the public mind a state of stupefied saturation, accompanied by symptoms of atony and imbecility." Italian newspapers, on the other hand, were henceforth free to serve the nation.

The argument, as Mr. Pynk points out, is sophistical, but the point is clear. To serve the nation's cause may be the greatest freedom; and, conversely, it is a necessity of the nation's life, if it is to be lived in fulness, to enlist the spiritual forces of the nation in its cause. As things are now, the state concerns itself only with its schools, and this only in a limited degree. It supports them and in principle controls them, but in practice it follows here also the rule of *laissez faire.* It is considered to be the function of the school to infuse facts and figures, but to shy away from anything that savors of propaganda or indoctrination, with the result that if the student acquires any social outlook, or *Weltanschauung,* he gets it haphazard from sources which are quite independent of the state. This, Mr. Pynk insists, will not do. "The business of the schools," he says, "is not merely to give knowledge and to exercise intelligence, but also, with conscious purpose and with more deliberate intention than at present, to instil definite ideas about the important movements of our time and to create a mental and moral attitude in harmony with the best aspirations of the state."

But the state cannot afford to narrow its concern to schools alone. It is perilous to exclude from its purview all the educational and formative influences which are at work outside the school. That was well enough when these influences were more negligible; it will not do now that they are become paramount. Such influences as go out from the printed page, the cinema, and the wireless are constant and all but universal forces in shaping the public mind and character. Not only that, such potent forces are entrusted to commercial interests which are free, if they so will, to exploit our appetites for what is cheap, sensational, and morbid; to prey upon human nature at its lowest levels, where the greatest profits are; and so to vitiate the atmosphere in which we live and move and have our being.

Mr. Pynk speaks out in strong and sweeping terms—too sweeping, perhaps. Because an agency, let us say a publishing house, is mercenary in the sense that it must balance its ledger or go out of business, it is not necessarily venal in its purpose or its effect. In fact there are many commercial agencies in this field which aim definitely at the improvement of the public mind and taste. Mr. Pynk would, no doubt, admit that gratefully. He is thinking of the profiteers who in increasing numbers "go," as he puts it, "like serpents on their bellies"; and he is condemning in round terms a state of affairs where, except for schools and churches (and in England the radio), we place all the instrumentalities of public instruction, entertainment and recreation in the hands of commercial agencies, which all too often become venal agencies, trafficking in the things of the spirit as others traffic in oil or soap or patent medicines.

Our English liberal realizes that he is on dangerous ground when he proposes a greater degree of regimentation in the things of the mind. He is painfully aware of what an ill-considered censorship may do in the hands of a bigoted minority. A control, to be salutary for a larger freedom, must grow out of a national awakening, a mobilization of our best intelligence and conscience against "the disintegrating and demoralizing forces now playing upon the mob mind. While not adopting the partisan position, the state will have to enforce a certain standard of honesty and sincerity in things which affect public thought and sentiment: it will have to make a lack of social conscience in literature and art . . . a crime of the first magnitude: it will have to stop the trade in brains to be used to pander to the crudest desires of the mob. And in the capacity of national trustee of education it will have to do what it can, both inside and outside the school, to set up standards of public opinion, and to prevent the spread of ideas which all intelligent people would condemn as pernicious."

I have given the last paragraph in the author's own words. Perhaps his uneasiness about what he terms "the mob" is not without its snobbishness. A Jacksonian might retort that the masses of the people are entitled to take their pleasures in their own way. Every man to his own taste, in a democratic country. But it is not so simple as all that. The question is not whether good taste and bad taste shall be allowed to rub shoulders in a live-and-let-live comradeship, but whether good taste can survive a mass production which caters to the mob instincts and appetites that lurk in every one of us. There is an interesting scene in Plato's *Republic,* where a man, taking an early morning walk outside of Athens, catches sight of some dead bodies just beyond the city walls, flung there by the public executioner to rot. There are other things to see: beauty everywhere in the clean dawn, the mountains violet-crowned, the blue sea whitening against the rocks, the Parthenon upon the sacred hill. His better nature tells him to avert his gaze from the one blot upon the scene. He is pulled this way and that. But in the end his morbid instinct wins the day; he rushes to where the bodies lie; stoops over the gruesome spectacle; and with rough fingers thrusts his eyelids wide apart, saying in disgust: "Look, damn you, look!"

We are all, I suppose, like that. And to "let freedom ring" too freely may be to enslave "the better angels of our nature."

I have taken time to review particularly the last half of Mr. Pynk's book because it is an admirable attempt to warn liberalism against the many crimes that are committed in its name, and because his observations, in so far as they are just, are as pertinent to our country as to the England for which he writes.

Certainly what he says is pertinent to our schools. I do not wish to add to the deluge of criticism, much of it venal in motive, which has threatened to drown appreciation of our schools. Beyond question, they are the most sincere and honest institutions which we have, and the most devoted to the public welfare. Yet we who teach must admit that the work of our hands has not matched our expectations. For one thing, we have not disturbed appreciably the citizenship which bases itself on the principle of everybody for himself. We have not, in other words, contributed effectively to the formation of a national accord, a national *esprit de corps,* a national culture.

Two influences mainly—the one akin to the other—have militated against this. The first is that of an excessive individualism in teaching, which has been accentuated by the extreme specialization and fragmentation of instruction. A college of liberal arts, for example, finds it difficult to produce a unified, liberal culture, whose faculty are dissociated by their deeper intellectual interests and associated only by a common participation in the superficial things of life. The second influence is that of an excessive regard for the individualities of the taught, which is part of our liberal tradition. We shy at discipline and anything which savors of regimentation. The youth in school who was excused from marching with his mates because he had a sacred rhythm all his own is an extreme case in point. We are reluctant to trespass upon the freedom of the mind to expand in its own way; and in our teaching we tend merely to analyze unrelated patches in the field of knowledge, leaving it to the immature student to make his own synthesis—which he seldom if ever does. We are all acquainted with the professor type who lectures with cold impartiality on every side of a question, defying his students to guess what his own personal feelings are. His purpose is to teach the students how to think, not what to think—a good principle if not pushed too far. But this virtue may turn out to be a vice. Where there is no vision, the students perish. The great teacher is one who sees his subject in relation to the world in which we live and is able to transmute the fragmentary substance with which he deals in the alembic of a contagious personality into the stuff of which attitudes of mind and character are made; he is in the good sense of the word a propagandist.

And let it not be forgotten that the American teacher is engaged in the making of Americans. In this regard, we have been drifting with an aimlessness which is no longer tolerable and now, fortunately, no longer excusable. Again I make grateful mention of the *Charter for the Social Sciences,* which, at last, after all these years of confusion, represents a deliberate, thoughtful concert of national opinion as to a proper Americanism to be taught in our schools. It is not the work of school men alone, but it is primarily of and by as well as for the schools, and should serve not only as a Magna Charta of principles but as a declaration of independence against minorities which have attempted and will attempt to dragoon our schools into teaching a shallow and spurious nationalism— a patriotism based upon distortions of history. Such patriotism may be better than none at all, but there is a larger and deeper patriotism which is able to see the weak spots and even the ugly spots in our national experience and yet say with the poet, "O Beautiful, My Country."

The schools can be depended on to do their part. There is a public conscience in the teaching profession, a "constant and continuous searching for the thing that is better," which will prevail unless the venal efforts now being put forth to degrade not only the economic status but the social status of the teacher succeed to the point of making teaching, not an honored profession, but a menial occupation.

But the schools cannot well do one thing while other institutions which are perhaps more potent in the long run do quite another thing, especially in the United States where, for example, the printing press, the radio, and the moving picture theatres are so universally pervasive and persuasive in their influence.

We have had recently a lively discussion of the freedom of the press, much of which has ignored the true quality of freedom. Were Jefferson living today, I imagine that he would modify his enthusiasm for an unbridled press as being more important than government itself. We have the best and the worst newspapers in the world, and many of the worst have large circulations and tremendous influence upon the mass mind. It is impossible to generalize about the situation by and large, except to say that only in rare instances does the American newspaper lay sufficiently to heart its grave responsibility as an instrument of education. It should cause no just offense to our journalist friends to remark that they are blessed with the freedom to present a balanced picture of the world from day to day and not to play up its aberrations and perversions. Indeed, the piling up of crimes and scandals on the front page has ceased, from sheer repetition, to be sensational—has ceased, that is to say, to be "news"; but, what is more important, it has tended to create a confusion of mind as to what is normal and what is abnormal. Those of us who have matured in an atmosphere less affected by the printed page are not misled, though we are often disheartened, by this "sensationalism," but we cannot escape the question whether the daily contemplation of distorted images of human life by immature and unreflecting minds does not distort their own outlook upon life. If our news agencies would be less avid for news in the Charles A. Dana definition of that term, and would scour the

country and the world for "whatsoever things
are honest, whatsoever things are just, whatsoever things are pure, whatsoever things are
lovely and of good report" and duly feature
these, what news that would be—what refresh-
ing news, what tonic news, what good news!

As to the radio, one recalls Seneca's depressing
observation that there is no invention, potent
for our good, which we do not turn to our
harm. It is no less than a national misfortune
that this gift of the gods with its marvelous pos-
sibilities for wholesome popular recreation and
instruction is in the United States a private
enterprise for profit, monopolized largely by
hucksters who every week day and every holy
day pitch their entertainments to the lowest
level of the popular taste and even below that
level. There are, let us be thankful, beautiful
exceptions; but a single dose of the banal imbecilities which form the average evening programme should be enough to speed on its way
the bill now before Congress whose stated purpose is "to develop a system of broadcasting for
the United States that will most effectively promote the interests of listeners and the national
interests of the United States."

But more important even than the printed page or the wireless in its effect upon the public mind and taste is the photoplay. In this field again one must generalize with caution. Some plays are excellent; some salacious, pandering to the "peeping Tom" in us; most are without positive qualities, being merely inane and flat, lacking both the salt and the spice of life.

It is not open to question that the Hollywood films have done more than anything else to create a distorted view of American life and character in foreign countries. We have not been so well agreed as to their effect upon the American audience. Mr. Will H. Hays has insisted that the picture industry has a moral ideal —that it is as much concerned for "that sacred thing, the mind" in its formative period as is "the best clergyman or the most inspired teacher of youth." On the other hand, Nicholas Murray Butler has charged that the movie as now directed and controlled "cannot but be destructive of ideals that have proved to be wholesome and worthy of preservation."

Fortunately, a searching study, financed by the Payne Fund, has been carried on during the past four years on the effects of this form of recreation upon our youth, and a summary of the results of this investigation is now available in a book, *Our Movie Made Children*. From this, it appears that practically all our boys and girls are habitués of the movie theatre, and are positively influenced for good or for ill by the types of plays which they witness. Such studies and the public conscience which they awaken will no doubt be salutary. Equally salutary, and very heartening to believers in democracy, is the discovery on the part of film producers that their patrons are not morons, and that it pays to play up, not down, to the public taste. There appeared recently in the *Saturday Evening Post* (which can hardly be dismissed as a high-brow journal) a very significant cartoon which pictures the office room of "Salacious Films, Inc." In the office are two men, their faces manifestly unlit by the idealism of which Mr. Hays speaks. Business is obviously at a standstill. One of them is reading with stupid consternation a news page with the sensational headline, "Clean Shows Making Box Office History." The other, his face twisted with pained incredulity, ejaculates, "It's against human nature," as he gazes through the window across the street where a great throng of eager people, young and old, are pushing and crowding into a theatre where *Little Women* is being played.

I have been greatly interested in the impression made by *Little Women* both in England and at home. A thoughtful critic in *The London Observer*, writing about this picture under the caption, *The Rediscovery of America*, found it, to use his own words, "a complete joy . . . simple, sincere to the spirit of a gorgeously sentimental race . . . frankly and unashamedly American, not Hollywood American, not New York American, but American in the sense of well over a hundred million folks earning their daily bread." Among our own audiences there was something of the same wistfully grateful feeling. It was like coming back after a long absence to the home of one's childhood. There were the emancipated few (or should I say the deracinated few?) who scorned its utter lack of sophistication—its sentimentalism; but the many of my generation found in it a happy rediscovery of America—of an America fading from our memory, but not lost to us, for it is in and of our very blood.

The rediscovery of America, the unending rediscovery of America—that is the plea and burden of these lectures. Spengler is wrong about America, but right in saying that a people preoccupied with getting and spending cannot be, save in the shallowest sense, a nation. For the time being, it should not trouble us that our economic interest is paramount. We must first of all have bread. But man cannot live, and nations cannot live, by bread alone.

To root ourselves firmly in our soil and our tradition, to cherish and enrich our culture, to create a spiritual climate in which our hearts and minds shall be really free to grow and expand to the fulness of their powers—that and nothing less is the challenge to our nation now that it must adventure anew and "nobly save or meanly lose the last best hope of earth."

www.ingramcontent.com/pod-product-compliance
Lightning Source LLC
Chambersburg PA
CBHW030655270326
41929CB00007B/375